DOWNLOAD THE UPDATED VERSION OF YOURSELF

Kenyatta Sammons

OwnYourLife ™ Publishing

OwnYourLife ™ Publishing
Clinton NC
www.ownyourlifetm.com

ISBN 13: 978-0-578-39614-9

Cover Design: Darwin | YOUTBOOKS
Cover Photo: Kenyatta Sammons
Edited By: Joseph Editorial Services, LLC.
Consulting: Tamika Melvin

This is a work of non-fiction. The characters are real and refer to actual stories based on real-time and real events.

Copyright © 2022 by Kenyatta Sammons

All rights are reserved. No part of this book may be reproduced in any manner whatsoever without written permission, except in the case of brief quotations embodied in critical articles and reviews.

Table of Contents

Introduction v
Chapter 1: Self-Reflection 1
Chapter 2: Resetting 7
Chapter 3: The 30-Day Mental Diet 13
Chapter 4: Check Engine Light 18
Chapter 5: In Case of a Fire, Take the Stairs 22
Chapter 6: Delta 27
Chapter 7: Keeping Company With God 35
Chapter 8: Crack Your Egg to Get to Your Yolk 41
Chapter 9: Get Up and Open the Curtains 47
Chapter 10: Affirmations 54
Conclusion 61
About the Author 62
Notes 63

Introduction

I never realized I had a choice in the way I viewed myself and how I was operating in life. For a long time, I was wandering through life thinking my years were free for me to do what I wanted. Or so, I was told. I had no purpose, no meaning, and the only drive I had came from alarms going off, alerting me to get up and start my day. To wake up and dive into the morning routine.
Brush my teeth.
Wash my face.
Get dressed.
Eat breakfast.
Start my day.
I lived a life in the demands of someone else. One day I asked myself, "Is this the meaning of my life? To work pay bills and hit repeat?"

What about living a life under my own esteem? Not having to answer to anyone. I pictured that being better than what I was doing. But there was no need for me to think I could own my life without owning myself first.

I enjoy being outside gazing at trees, flowers, and birds flying in the sky. I love to laugh, and I love food made with love. I love the comfort the nighttime brings, and I enjoy going for walks. I love catching sunrises, sunsets and being in the water. I escape to another world when I listen to music and without God, I am nothing.

What is it about change, that no matter what I must endure I still want more of it? I find more about who I am when I am uncomfortable. When I remain stagnant and not allow myself to be exposed to different things, I create a foundation that teaches me to play it safe when it comes to my life. I like the challenge of being radical and going against all the odds and believing that God and I can build a life that is bigger than who I am. To see life from another perspective I must gain the courage to do something different. I cannot stay within the same frame of mind or do the same things and expect a new outcome. Are you willing to let God turn you upside down, so you can gain a new way of seeing yourself and life? *Remember life is like monopoly game, to gain you must be willing to lose.* Life is about failing and getting back up. My life can be as grand as I want it to be but without ACTION, FIGHT, and CONSISTENCY, I build no life at all. I remain average when God created me to be exceptional.

Two important things I want you to know, it is okay to make mistakes; you don't need to stay stuck on the errors for too long. Instead, take circumstances as learning lessons and move on, especially if it is out of your control. Secondly, if you have a feeling or an idea that does not make sense to those around you. Have enough nerve to do YOU against all the odds. Sometimes it must be you and God that believe in you, and you must get comfortable with that.

I know you may want others to believe in you the way you do but it's not their responsibility. Trust me you will bring yourself added stress that you don't need. You have beautiful instincts and gifts that make up who you are. Don't stray from those things because others may not accept them, be and stand bold in who you are and love you first. Always bring your energy into spaces instead of waiting to see how others embrace you. You were not made to fit it but born to stand out.

This book will allow you to listen in on a conversation that I am having with the little girl on the inside of me. There will be moments where she speaks but I am the one she needed in her corner when she was going through life and didn't have the guidance, love, and support she needed. The little girl down on the inside of me had to endure things and could no longer wait to be rescued by someone. You will be listening in on me being the teacher to my broken self and the things that I did to download the upgraded version of myself.

Enough with being defined by past mistakes, old habits, and being labeled by those that do not even know who they are. The "just getting by" lifestyle is outdated and YOU have too much to offer to be just getting by. I do hope you take a leap of faith for what you desire and believe that you can download the updated version of yourself. It is within you to hit the reset button on your life, own your life, and be in the driver's seat. But you must be willing to apply the action, stay in the fight, and remain committed to you.

I have chosen to notice who I am and see the beauty in what I possess. I have wings that are ready to be spread open. I have been quiet and shy for most of my life—a stay in the background kind of person. But once I began laying in pipelines such as Eric Thomas, Dr. Thema, Iyanla Vanzant, Sarah Jakes, Willis Kinnear, and Bishop Jakes, things began to shift. God began to open my ears, heart, mind, and soul. I had enough with playing it safe, and I was willing to go through what I had to, to see a different life than what I was seeing. I had to realize that feeding my mind was my first step. Applying action and remaining committed followed.

If I continued to be unstable, saying I was going to do this or that, and never doing anything, I was telling myself that I was fine with being cheated on and my word held no weight. It was time to put an end to that and begin holding myself accountable.

Continue with me on this journey and remember the process of finding who you are does not come overnight but no matter what it takes, **STICK IT OUT.** We all must endure unpleasant experiences and though we have gone through life experiences. One of the greatest gifts you have is Time. God allows Time to move forward, which means you must choose to move forward from anything that's anchored you down. You can get up again, and YOU can own your life.

Chapter 1
Self-Reflection

To understand reflection, you must understand self. Whenever you reflect on something, you are taking a moment to think about it carefully. Self is the complete being of you. So how do you self-reflect if you don't deem yourself to be complete? Start looking inside of yourself.

Where do your roots stem from?
Why do you respond the way you respond?
Do you respect yourself?

These are some questions to ask yourself while you are reflecting. You want to self-reflect when you can have some quiet time for yourself and away from distractions. When is the last time you thought about yourself? Avoiding self-reflection comes at a cost. It is a must that you check in with yourself because you always want to be aware of how you are feeling, thinking, what's around you, who is influencing you and how you take care of yourself. If you don't take time to care for you, don't look for someone else to do so.

Self-reflection is the habit of deliberately paying attention to your thoughts, emotions, decisions, and behaviors (Wignall, 2019). So, we see that self-reflection is more than standing in front of a mirror and looking at yourself. You must obtain a habit of standing up to yourself.

To analyze your thoughts, emotions, decisions, and behaviors.

The idea of changing your life around comes as a thought first and is followed up by looking into yourself to see the areas that could use some reconstructing.

If you don't take time to self-reflect. How will you know what you need? Isn't it time to be complete with you? Isn't it time to look at you from a place that is desperate for change? You deserve to BE and go after anything that builds you up. You are beautiful, alive, and bold. Self-reflection will lead you to seeing yourself differently if you put in the time and effort to do so.

Self-reflection can be ugly before you see the beauty in it because it involves a process of looking at who you have become, what influences you, how mistakes and staying connected to the past have shaped your life, and what you have allowed to be acceptable. Without self-reflection how do you know who you truly are? Stop being oblivious to you.

Growing up I was skinny, and people would say, "Girl, you need to gain some weight." And eventually, I did. But I guess I gained too much in their eyes because I began getting picked on for the weight gain. Which led to me feeling bad. But I had to realize that I was teaching myself to be okay with being controlled by others' opinions of me. So even though I would go to the gym and workout, I was working out with wrong intentions. If I was going to lose weight, I needed to lose weight for myself and not anyone else. And though I did not like what I was making acceptable in my life, I knew I needed to change, so one day I came to myself and said, *if you don't lose this weight for you, you will never lose it. Stop worrying about other people's opinions of you. IT DOES NOT MATTER!* And once I made that mental loop up in my mind, I refused to feel bad when it was brought up again.

I felt way better. And when I got into losing weight and going to the gym, I made it clear to myself that I was doing this for me.

Can you try to believe that there is another version of you awaiting to be revealed? Can you imagine for a moment that you are the gift wrapped up? Self-reflection must and can only begin with you. You don't have to deal with anything that makes you feel less than who you are. Trust me, I did it for years and now that I can see myself, it is one of the greatest gifts God has revealed to me. Discover a new truth about who you are and who you can become. Is it the fear of changing that keeps you in the same lane for years or are you comfortable? Take a moment to answer for yourself, and if it is neither, write down precisely what it is.

"Do not conform to the pattern of this world but be transformed by the renewing of your mind. Then you will be able to test and approve what God's will is—his good, pleasing, and perfect will," (Romans 12:2 NIV).

If you want to see anything differently, it must first come from a new mind. There is no need to begin the journey and still choose what old things you want to keep. You can give yourself a clean slate. A fresh mind shifts perspectives and provides light to dreams, unique desires, change in attitudes, provides courage, welcomes peace, opens eyes and hearts, and so much more. Enough with blaming people for the way you act or blaming the devil for dreadful things happening. Sometimes you are the blame for your mess. Remember in everything you do, you always have a choice, and it is your responsibility to pick up in the areas of your life.

If God is a growing God, then so are you. If it is not in His will for you to make a home out of junk, then it should not be in your will either. You must work at self-reflecting. You cannot self-reflect for one day and say, "Okay I did it." Remember self-reflecting is a habit. **I chose** to position myself to see every day as a new day. If something happened yesterday that bothered me, I spent time before bed reflecting on it and I chose to clear myself from the issue before going to sleep. I no longer wanted to be consumed with the issues that I dealt with on Monday and drag those issues into Tuesday. I knew I would never understand the gifting in having daily bread if I was continuing to bring problems from yesterday into a new day. You must speak and encourage yourself. Some may think that speaking to yourself is unorthodox but you must do what is best for you. If I find myself not being able to have clarity on a situation, I hand it over to God because I trust that He knows what to do with my situation.

The choice was up to me to choose a different route and began to lay down new mental loops in my mind. I started reading, listening to sermons, podcasts, and motivational speakers. I had to get plugged into certain people, and it seemed as if the more I chose a different route, the more God began showing of Himself.

"Whoever sows sparingly will also reap sparingly, and whoever sows generously will also reap generously," (2 Corinthians 9:6 NIV). This scripture is proof that God will work and meet you wherever you are. My harvest was based on what I sowed. If I sow poorly, I will reap poorly. If I sow generously, I will reap generously.

My first job was working at Taco Bell. I was excited to be working there because I was beginning to make money. After about a year, I believe my appetite was changing. I was looking for something that gave me more drive, elevated my money, and I did not want to get comfortable. I knew those things. But what about the things I dealt with in secret? Still fighting with my past, making excuses, and playing the blame game. I had no control over my mind, and I walked around for years like that.

I had to get past the surface of seeing myself and deal with the things underneath. Yes, I desired change but if I did not change within myself first, I would still be walking around dealing with things in secret. I had to sit with all my doubts, insecurities, worries, and anxieties and figure out why I was okay with allowing these things to control my life. There is no war like having a war within yourself. I had to let the toxic thoughts of my past go, relationships that still represented the old me, and wash my hands with ignoring red flags. Turmoil was making a home in my mind, and I had to let it go. I could no longer be here and there at the same time with myself. It was very exhausting, and I knew If I could focus on what makes me, I could win the fight.

I wanted to be where God saw me, which matters more than remaining the same. You must get in a place where you learn how to trust yourself. Any noun that is not for you, LET IT GO! If I cannot trust myself, how can I look to anyone else for trust? You do not have to be two different people. Own being you authentically. It is not about attracting people. It is about being the best version you can be. Know your why, while you self-reflect. Remember everything has meaning. God knows everything about you. And He wants you to renew everything you have been through. Isn't it your time to be renewed?

If I did not choose to take the time to find out who I was, I would still be living life for others and what they thought was best for me. But after a while, I began to ask myself *is this how you are going to conduct YOUR life?* The answer was NO! I would have continued to teach myself that living life with chains hooked to me was okay.

Self-reflection allows you to look within and ask yourself what are the things that build you up? Do you know what brings you joy, peace, new understandings, and a sense of purpose? Or are you okay with doing things that do not allow you to step outside your comfort zone?

When you trust the process and image the shift in what self-reflection can look like for you, THINK BIG! You can change at any moment. So why not begin RIGHT NOW?

Writing Prompts

What is holding you back? List five things that are holding you back from where you want to be:

1._____
2._____
3._____
4._____
5._____

Now, serve each one an eviction notice. Make it clear that today is the last day you will allow any of these things to hold you back.

_____
_____
_____
_____
_____
_____
_____
_____
_____
_____

Affirmation

I embrace self-reflection
when
what is reflected doesn't add value to my spirit any longer
I let it go

Chapter 2
Resetting

To step into resetting, you must self-reflect first. Resetting is an important part of the journey but it means nothing if you decide to carry old ways into your reset. Do not reset an old you. Self-reflecting is meant for you to declutter and see yourself differently. Resetting is the next step because you have figured out what is good for you and what is not. Once that is sorted, now you step onto new ground and begin to walk in what you have gained.

It is not in transitioning to resetting that I found to be difficult. It is maintaining the new position that comes as a challenge because when you have been programmed for so long to do things a certain way, coming out from under that is not easy. But everything is not meant to be easy, so you must come to a place where you are not operating out of your feelings, but you are consciously making the decision to say no matter what, I will stay on track with becoming and attracting all that is for me.

This is what my life was looking like before I chose to step into my reset. JACKED UP (LOL). The Binomial Theorem $(x+a)^n = \sum_{k=0}^{n} \binom{n}{k} x^k a^{n-k}$. It was time I see myself as simple as. $a^2 + b^2 = c^2$.

I started out not knowing who I was, which led to me trying to fit in with people when God made me to stand out. I was not taking my healing journey seriously, so I was still attracting what was not good for me. I was a walking mess. It did not matter how pretty I was on the outside, I carried garbage on the inside. Are you pretty garbage? Take it from me, if you go back and accept things less than who you are, you forfeit the game of life. Life is not meant to be ran off emotions. So, I told myself that no matter what, I would not back slide again. And slowly but surely, I kept my word. Enjoy the process. And look forward to people misunderstanding you.

I worked for a mental health company between the ages of twenty-one and twenty-four. I grew some skin working in that field and enjoyed my work during those years. I love how I was able to grow and more importantly, make an impact in someone else's life. One day I no longer felt happy going to work. Of course, I tried to ignore it but I couldn't fight what I was feeling on the inside.

It came out of nowhere, and I sat on the feeling for about two weeks. After two weeks I decided to face my boss and express that I would be leaving. Once I left the company I was in a fog. I was taking jobs with lesser pay. I cleaned doctor's offices, drove for Uber and Lyft, and did a babysitting gig. I remember seeing a psychic because I could not rationalize what was happening. *Why would I leave a job, take lesser pay, and add on more jobs to compensate for the main one I already had?*

It was because it was time to embark on another journey and God had something else in mind for me. Some days I didn't know if I was coming or going but I kept moving forward because I trusted the nudge over the security the job provided.

Even though I wanted to understand what was happening, it was not for me to understand because everything is in His control. NOT MINE. I knew He was tugging at me, so it was time to pick up and move on.

As humans, we try to explain things and have things make sense before moving into another dimension of our lives. God knows what's best for us, so why not try to get out of your way and allow Him to guide you while being blindfolded? Remember life is not meant for you to remain the same. Get plugged into people that are going higher with their lives and are radical enough to set ambitious standards and achieve them. Do not look for validation. If you do not have anyone around that can relate to you fixing yourself, REMAIN IN YOUR TUNNEL VISION! You do not have to chase anything or anyone because you attract what you are. Do what you need to do so you can see yourself at your fullest potential.

The small things that I began shifting were allowing me to see myself in a new way. The best thing for you is to be authentic to who you are. I began making myself laugh, I began journaling, I liked being alone, I began yearning to listen to a sermon at least once a week. There were some moments I would be listening to music, and I would quickly turn it to go for a sermon or a motivational speech. I was developing new desires. Sometimes old thoughts came by to visit and I wanted to do things that tied me to who I used to be. But I fought my way through it, and when I felt as if aiming to be better was not overpowering the old version of myself, I asked God to help me because it was not worth going backward.

You will have groanings during your reset, beautiful. Take a moment to breathe and get back focused. If you can get through the war of having the old voice on one shoulder and the new voice on the other, that is a win. The thing about mental wars is, they come without warning. I had to begin speaking down on old thoughts that were trying to rise.

I started telling my old thoughts to leave a voicemail. I stayed reminding myself that I was not my past. I will fear no evil, I am free and alive, I am moving forward, I will not be defeated. Listen, YOU MUST ENCOURAGE YOURSELF! You must be willing to get into the ring of your life and when those old thoughts rise, because they will rise, it is you who must show them who is the boss. Though you have no control over the thoughts that come into your mind you do have a say with the amount of time you give to them. The time is now to fight for you.

The number eleven-eleven, "Resonates with new beginnings, motivation to move forward, taking inspired action, achieving success, independence, and leadership. Now is a great time to embrace your unique qualities- your individuality- JUST DO YOU!" (Burnett, 2021). This is one of the numbers I began seeing a lot and I had no idea why.

I never would have gained the notion to investigate the number if a good friend of mine had not had a conversation with me. I would have never known my angels were trying to get in contact with me but when she said it to me, it began to resonate. I went to South Carolina from June 21st through June 25th of 2021. My room number was eleven-eleven and during that week, I kept catching eleven-eleven. Even throughout the months going forward, I began seeing three-three-three, two-two-two, four-four-four, five-five-five. All of it for me was divine timing.

You should give yourself thirty days to do something different from your routine. Doing the same old thing will lead you to living in revolving doors. You are going around and around and never taking the opportunity to get off. Resetting is uncomfortable, but the process is well worth it. It is time for you to break into new territory. Why not you?

Don't forget about renewing your mind. I used to be quick to tell someone I was grown. But I was referencing my age as if age defines my maturity. Age does not define how mature you are. How you feed your mind and plant new mental loops down in your mind, is what defines maturity. A new mind leads to a new way of thinking. With grace, failing and getting back up, commitment, action and YOU, you will reset and become a new version of yourself.

I want something to resonate within you.
I want to be the match that lights you on fire
so you go within yourself and begin to dig out
what God has placed in you.

God gives us a DAILY dose of new grace and new mercy. Knowing this led me to believe that we have a unique opportunity every day to discover something new and a new way of being within ourselves. If I take the opportunity to unite God's fresh grace with discovering more of who I am, I am making a statement in my life, and I'm telling the old version of myself that a new version is on the rise. And there is only room for one version.

"Thou madest him to have dominion over the works of thy hands; thou hast put all things under his feet," (Psalms 8:6 KJV).

This scripture serves as a reminder for us all. God has already blessed us with everything we need. It is up to you to do what needs to be done so you can see everything that you are destined for

Words are POWERFUL! If you tell yourself you can't do something more than likely, you won't because you are what you tell yourself. But if you began changing the way that you speak to yourself you will be surprised at how things can change. God won't magically make you whole. You must be willing to put in some action of your own. Listen, God does not do all the work. So, if that is what you're waiting for, GOOD LUCK! God is for partnerships. When you begin discovering who you are, you begin trusting yourself in a new way. Resetting leads you to live in the alignment of what is rightly yours.

Writing Prompts

What is holding you back from resetting? List five things that are holding you back from where you want to be:

1._____
2._____
3._____
4._____
5._____

Now, serve each one an eviction notice. Make it clear that today is the last day you will allow any of these things to hold you back.

_____
_____
_____
_____
_____
_____
_____
_____
_____
_____
_____

Affirmation

I begin resetting myself now
my words and I are power
I AM the infinite being
God created me to be

CHAPTER 3

THE 30-DAY MENTAL DIET

On September 30th, 2021, I saw a shooting star for the first time while being at work. At the time, I was working at Home Depot in Upper Marlboro, Maryland. My manager called for a break and instead of me going to sit down somewhere in the store or my car, I decided to go outside and sit on the ground. It was cold out, but it was a beautiful night. I sat on the ground and began centering myself. I began engaging in a few breathing exercises, wrapping my arms around myself, and thanking God for showing His goodness to me. I'm looking up in the night sky, gazing with beautiful stars, and while I was in the moment, a shooting star shot across the sky. I remember screaming with joy and having a huge smile on my face. And it was in that moment that I realized God was giving me a sneak peek of what it looks like to have a sound mind.

The 30-Day Mental Diet is a book I read by Willis Kinnear. I encourage you to get a copy. Not only did it enhance my mental loops, but it allowed me to hold myself accountable for something other than going to work. The book consists of thirty daily thought routines and exercises that strengthen the mind. Once I started the book, I did not understand some of the readings, but I kept at it until I did. I was reading the book for a few months in a row, and it appeared to me that I was getting a new understanding each time. I knew I was wanting to make up my mind with new things. I chose to realize that it was okay to not understand something new. I gain nothing by giving up and I cheat myself with even thinking that's an option.

The book is instructed to be read daily. One day the reading slipped my mind. I was on day six and I read day six. But day seven came and I missed it. So, I had to start over to day one. Yes, I could have said, "Well, I can skip one day and keep going. But I was no longer in the business of CHEATING MYSELF. Some days I didn't feel like reading, but it was not up to my feelings. It was up to me being accountable. Having the thoughts of, *you can miss one day,* or *if you skip a day its fine,* were old teachings rising. And it was showing me what I was training myself to be okay with it. If I was on day fourteen and I missed day fifteen, all I could do was sigh, because I knew I was going right back to day one.

After about four times of me going through the cycle of missing days, I was fed up. It was time I prioritize my reading. I did not have that much going on, where I could not set aside fifteen minutes and complete the reading.

What is something that you have been putting off that needs your attention?

Having excuses and allowing your feelings to be the head of your life **is dangerous.** You're not always going to feel like doing things. Tell your feelings, YOU are the boss of your life. You will never accomplish anything if your feelings are in control. Why not start today on holding yourself accountable? Yes, you may fail your way to the finish line but see the lessons along the way. Lessons shape you into becoming a better person. You can change anytime you decide to do so for yourself. You are the author, director, and CEO, of your life. It is up to you to do whatever it takes to own your life to the fullest. You can began starting off with something as small as reading a book to get you in the rhythm of holding yourself accountable. Never give up on molding yourself into becoming better.

I want to incorporate a few things that stood out to me during the diet. Day four's title reads, "Learn to Think Constructively." "It is necessary that you think in a constructive manner," (Kinnear, 1963). From reading the title, I take that I cannot allow anything to consume my mind. And that I can LEARN to think in a constructive way. If I can get into a place where my thoughts are constructive, what kind of life can I build for myself? My curiosity was piqued and I figured if I could learn to think constructively, I could govern my mind better.

What do you gain from reading the title?

I understand that I cannot control thoughts that come into my mind. But I do believe daily habits play a part. And I can choose how much effort I give to unnecessary thoughts. Unannounced thoughts come by and visit but I have learned to quickly send them away. Depending on the situation, my mind could roam about things and before I knew it, forty minutes had passed. Unannounced thoughts were robbing me of valuable time. I am so thankful for all the content that Ms. Iyanla Vanzant provides. She taught me that when those unannounced thoughts rise, I can quickly speak out and command them to leave instead of allowing them to run rapidly in my mind.

You must be in a place in your mind where you want to see yourself better. It should no longer be acceptable to only live life to survive. The future is in God's hands, not in yours. I encourage you to make up your mind and strengthen yourself from within. The time is now to live and be free.

"Clear, consistent, affirmative patterns of thought will be creative of a fuller, richer life," (Kinnear,1963).

"A stagnant mind produces a stagnant body," (Kinnear, 1963).

"I open my mind, encompass the greatest good I can conceive, and without a question of doubt accept and act as if it were mine now-God does the rest," (Kinnear,1963).

There are so many delicious goods inside the book. I highly encourage you to purchase the 30-Day Mental Diet to gain access to them all. You invest in things that you like but what about the things that you need? I am not saying that you cannot invest in things that you like but there must be a balance. Give yourself thirty days to do something different. If what comes after the thirty days is worse than before you agreed to it, then go back to the way things were. But if not and you gain something that you did not previously have. Keep the faith and push forward.

Get into these search engines and plug into those who feed you. I recommend falling in love with reading. Expand the mind as much as you can to find more about what fuels you. The better you are, the better your life will be. You can begin now with gaining new knowledge and changing perspectives. Stop saying you don't have time for you because you do. I know you have been programmed to think a certain way for years and implementing new codes takes time but you can do this. If you needed more time, God would have granted it. Stop making excuses for yourself and do what needs to be done so that you can see how marvelous you are.

Writing Prompts

What will you do for the next thirty days to build up your mind? List two things:
1._____
2._____

Now, tell your feelings and distractions that you will remain committed. Write down what tried to stop you and how you overcame it.
_____
_____
_____
_____
_____
_____
_____
_____
_____
_____

Affirmation

I will do a new thing for thirty days
To be better than what I was yesterday
I will transform
into the highest being of myself

CHAPTER 4
CHECK ENGINE LIGHT

The check engine light is formally known as the malfunction indicator lamp. It illuminates when your vehicle's computer believes a problem could affect or is affecting your car's emissions control system. Our check engine light within our body comes on when we don't feel good. Suppose we were to catch a cold. Our body would begin feeling its symptoms. Some symptoms may be feeling weak, coughing, sneezing, or running nose. When does your check engine light come on within you, to let you know you need some service?

Take a moment and think about what is holding you back from running at your best self. This is what my check engine light was reading" procrastination, laziness, excuses, old stories, and justifying. I was adding nothing of value for myself. If I would have kept allowing my feelings to lead my life, I would have never grown. It was time to get the issues that were not allowing me to pivot, FIXED!

My check engine light would come on in my vehicle, but I knew nothing was wrong with my car. So, I would take a moment to scan myself. I would notice the areas that needed attention. I engaged in some self-reflecting on the areas and cleared them. And after about ten minutes or so, my check engine light would go off. Check in with yourself as much as possible. You and God are the only ones that know how you're always feeling. So why not spend quality time with you? One of the reasons the Holy Spirit began nudging at me to write this book was because it was time to do what fueled me. I never thought about writing a book until I started. I have always enjoyed writing, but a book never crossed my mind. My first version of what I thought was a book, my editor chewed it up and spit it out. I had nothing close to a book.

Oh, I was in my feelings big time. But I had to shake those feelings because she was critiquing my work, NOT ME. And had I not done previous work to not be led by my feelings, I would have never finished writing a book. THE DANGER OF BEING LED BY FEELINGS. While continuing to write, I began noticing that I was gaining a sense of purpose, commitment, and discipline. So, while producing the book I was learning lessons. There are lessons to be learned in everything you do in life. Always be attentive.

Check engine lights are designed to inform us that something needs attention. Check engine lights in your vehicle cannot tell you what the problem is. Until you can take it to an auto store or an auto shop and let a mechanic investigate why your light is on you will not know what the problem is. Sometimes it will take multiple steps to get things fixed. But if the dots are connecting along the process you can fix any problem.

God puts everything you need down on the inside of you. (HIDE AND GO SEEK). It took me years to stand on that because I was wrapped up in seeking validation from people instead of God. This check engine light stayed on for years. I would end up crying out to God to help me feel better when people made me feel like crap. So eventually, I got to a place where I flipped things around, and God and I gained a relationship. I no longer made Him my genie in a bottle nor treated Him like some maid. We became best friends.

I had more years of showing no commitment than I had being committed. I knew I could do all sorts of things, like opening a business, making candles, having a podcast, opening a shelter, and be on a billboard. But it was not about accomplishing everything at once. It was about sticking to something long enough and completing it. And writing my book taught me that. When working all day, getting off, getting some food, coming home, showering and relaxing is normalized for years, staying focused on something can be foreign. But I decided that no matter what. I was going to finish writing my book.

How long, how long, how long are you going to ride life with training wheels? You can have high hopes and live out a cornucopia life. But if you don't take off the training wheels and apply action, all it will be is high hopes. It is a must to get your check engine lights serviced. Get yourself together and stand on the discipline that is needed in your life. Don't you have things that you want to accomplish out of life? Yes, you will face obstacles along the way but don't allow the obstacles to eat you alive.

I love how God chose light to brighten everything up. I realized that it was a strategic choice. You can become overwhelmed when darkness is on you throughout life, allowing the darkness to overstay its welcome. It can and will wreak havoc in our lives, but I take a moment to thank God because when I choose to add some light to a dark circumstance at any time, darkness had to flee. I don't care what life has brought upon you that makes darkness feel like it can stay. You command light to come, and it will clear that darkness up. Sometimes it may take more than one command, but if you dare to believe, you can remove the darkness.

Writing Prompts

What check engine lights are you ignoring? List five of them that need servicing:
1._____
2._____
3._____
4._____
5._____

Now, serve each one an eviction notice. Make it clear that today is the last day you will allow any of these check engine lights to control your life.

_____
_____
_____
_____
_____
_____
_____
_____
_____
_____
_____

Affirmation

I will be in tune with my check engine lights
and give ME the highest quality
of service I can provide

Chapter 5
In Case of a Fire, Take the Stairs

I notice hotels post signs saying, "In case of a fire take the stairs." You do this because you get down the stairs faster than waiting on an elevator to open. When a fire occurs, you want to get away from the fire quickly. I wondered to myself, if I was applying the same urgency to overthinking, trying to impress people, hooking my feelings to the wrong people, and ignoring red flags what burns could I have avoided?

Look at your life and see the areas where you did not apply the urgency to get away quickly. Depending on the magnitude of the situation, you may have been left with first, second, or third-degree burns. It's time now that you stop waiting on that elevator; that person apologizing, wishing the situation never happened, and take your stairs. Get those things off you that keep you trapped. It's time to reveal your masterpiece because another life is waiting on you to arrive.

I was no longer interested with operating life from old, learned behaviors. I cannot change my past; I cannot drive myself crazy with "what ifs." I was tired of moving through life looking backward. I told myself it was time to stop pointing fingers and stop praying the same old prayers to God. No matter how I chose to reword the prayer, it was still the same. I must transition myself into creating something new. Waiting on the elevator to open was teaching me to wait on someone else to fix me. And I was running out of time waiting for someone else to grab my hand. So, I chose to grab my own. I can no longer dress up what is keeping me caged. I dare to believe that I can be free; I can fly high as an eagle in the sky.

Throughout life I was getting dressed in low self-esteem, not loving myself, worried about people's opinions, being afraid to speak up, not standing up for myself, and allowing unhealthy thoughts to control my day. I was putting my soul through fitting room exchanges instead of being rooted in myself. Coming up as a child, I was always the doer. And when you are always doing something for someone else, it comes at a cost.

Doing things for others leaves very little time to focus on you. I never said anything out loud, but I often wondered, *why am I the only one doing so much? Why can I never hang out with my friends? Why do I have to do all this work?* And for years, I did not know who I was or how to be me. Instead of figuring out for myself who I was, I tried fitting in.

Throughout my years, I was blaming my mom for sheltering me, mistreating me, and not showing me how to love. I was blaming my dad for not being around and not fighting for me. I was giving away too much power. I had to destroy all those mental loops because I refused to continue to make a life from what I had been through. It was time that my past and I break up because I wanted to get hooked to where I was going in life. Anything that keeps you from being the best that you can be is all in your head. If you can kill it in your head, it cannot throw its weight around in your life.

Caged minds develop blind perspectives that lead you to question your worth, your existence, the desire to end what you deal with, and tell yourself you're the only one dealing with issues.

I challenge you to no longer wait on the elevator of someone freeing you from the past. **ACT NOW.** Realize that the key you are looking for someone to give you is already in your possession, but it's buried under your history. You must get into a place where you want and choose to be free. IT WILL BE A PROCESS. Once you have found your key to unlock your mind be ready to tackle the things that will spill out before you. Begin dealing with one thing at a time.

Those things or situations that are tough for you to face, surrender to them and ask God to come in and help you. Because if you are not careful, your opposition will be the ruler of you and your life. Don't give in to telling yourself that it's too hard to deal with or you are not strong enough. Those thoughts come in as distractions, BUT YOU GOT THIS. Always remember God is a friend in trouble, and if you give Him those heavy burdens, He will take them from you. We are all fighting to overcome something. Stay focused on why you're overcoming your past. So, you can see yourself the best way possible.

God wants to do a new thing in you. He does not want you to walk around through life living in agony. There is a restoration process that is waiting for you. God without a doubt, can take something that is broken and restore it. When you come naked and say, "I'm tired of not living my life because of my past, I'm tired of blaming, I'm tired of crying, I'm tired of putting my hopes into people, I'm tired of feeling drained." I have shed many tears and there is no cry like the silent one to yourself.

Whatever your tired of, beautiful, you can be free from it. Get real with yourself and tell God everything. He already knows your troubles, so you don't have to be ashamed. I told Him I was here with all my baggage, and I want to be made new. I have done all that I can, and I need You. Old desires still aim to feed me, but I don't want that. I want to be in that place where I no longer thirst or hunger. I want to be made whole, restored, renewed, and I WANT TO LIVE. I was desperate. Are you desperate?

I had enough with gambling on God. God, if You get me through this, I won't do it again. Even though I meant it, I still found myself doing something else and I would be right back saying the same line to Him. So, I was carrying God like a bad drug and GOD WAS NOT "MY FIX." God is understanding, transformation, healing, wholeness, joy, peace, and light. He is "all of the above." You cannot use God only when you need Him. He is not your fishing rod. Throw Him out when you need Him to catch something, and when you're done, and He has helped you, you put Him away until next time. God is for relationship; partnership, and He has no care for the in and out.

There is no better time than right now to decide for yourself that you will clear out things that no longer have rights to stand in and with you. It is time to reconnect with yourself. Get rid of everything that keeps you further away from being home within yourself. Do away with putting off things until tomorrow. You are not God, and you cannot see further than the second you stand in. The next second, minute, or hour of the day are all beautiful blessings, and why would you waste precious time not being who God created you to be?

God wants you to have a fresh start at finding out for yourself who you are for YOU. It is crucial that against the odds, you see for yourself who you can become. So let us act and get serious about what truly makes us happy and perform at the highest level we can. No matter what comes your way in any form of distraction, fight it off and keep pushing until you reach your finish line.

Writing Prompts

What elevators are you waiting on to open? List five stairs that you need to take:

1._____
2._____
3._____
4._____
5._____

Now, serve each one an eviction notice. Make it clear that today is the last day you will allow any of these things to hold you back.

_____
_____
_____
_____
_____
_____
_____
_____
_____
_____
_____
_____

Affirmation

I can't burn and die yet
I have the option of taking the stairs
and I believe
another life that's bigger than my fire
waits for me

Chapter 6
DELTA

DELTA is the IV drip you need in your system. You always want to operate in life with nutrients that build you up. DELTA is Discover Evolve Learn Teach Adapt. How do you discover yourself? How do you evolve? How do you learn yourself? How can you teach someone what you have learned? How do you adapt? You don't have to wish on having a good life or being a better person. Both can happen, but you must be willing to apply **action**, **fight**, and **consistency**.

Discovering and evolving rustle together like autumn leaves, how do you evolve without discovering yourself? Take a moment and think about it. Next is the learning phase. You must learn yourself and learn from the choices you make. Never look for someone to teach you everything. It is not wise to not know anything for yourself. Adapting can be tricky because everything is a choice and if you don't discover, evolve, learn, and teach for **yourself**. You take the risk of adapting into what others have been displaying before you. You have your own life to live. And DELTA will work wonders for you if you work it.

Discovering who you are leads to your own awakening. If you don't discover who you are. You take the risk of walking in other people's shadows. You don't live every day to be stressed, worried, afraid, or concerning yourself with what will come tomorrow. Explore the beautiful person that you are. Aren't you worth discovering? You live and breathe with infinite possibilities at your disposal. DON'T WASTE YOU.

Know why you want to discover yourself before you begin. Finding YOU takes a lot of TIME. So, if you're not willing to work at discovering yourself. Don't look for someone else to discover you. Dig, and find the desires that lie within you. When you have been operating from a default setting for so long you must be the one to change the settings. And anytime you change what has already been **PRE**pared for you be ready to put in work and be uncomfortable. You must devote time to chase what lights you up. Don't worry about who likes it or not, continue to focus on you. People will tell you you're changing. But it's okay. This new setting is about getting yourself together. It's not about what others feel or think. Aren't you the gift wrapped up? God has designed you to discover yourself so that you can be true to you.

The beauty in discovering yourself leads to gaining new knowledge for yourself, and you can build up new things at any moment of your life. Expect people to not agree with what you are doing. If people are not aiming to put in work to find themselves and create a new system like you're aiming to do there is supposed to be confusion because the both of you are feeding on different levels. There is a chance you may feel like you're fighting to be heard and then left frustrated when you are not, or you want people to see the new you. But don't worry about being rewarded by people if you don't reward yourself first. God will allow you to run into the flock that is meant for you. But for now, the focus is on discovering you.

Begin taking yourself out on movie dates, dinner dates, going for walks, telling yourself you love you, exercising, hugging yourself. Fall in love with the discovery phase. It can be as bright as you want it to be and there are no limits when it comes to you. You will be able to see what you can and cannot put up with, how do you want to be spoken to, how you want to show up for yourself the list goes on and on. God designed you to be fruitful. And you cannot produce good fruit with bad seed. The more you discover you the more you find out who and what you are. The discovery phase is meant to be fun, challenging, insightful, interesting, and new. And I encourage you to not give up. When new truths are added, old ones are subtracted.

Evolving from what you have been discovering about yourself may lead to you having a low tolerance for distractions like social media, relationships, constantly being on your phone, drama, and family. You know what it's like dealing with low self-esteem, being afraid, staying quiet, letting what PEOPLE say define you and counting yourself short. But you must lay these things to rest so you can evolve. **Evolving is a process**. Now you sit with what you have discovered about yourself, what needs to be changed, and how do you change it.

Know why you're changing and always change for **you**. You are the only one that can live your life. You don't have to deal with anything you don't want to deal with. For years you have been taught and shown that you do, but you don't. Don't be the one to damage yourself because you know and see the things you need to evolve from and not change them. You're not always going to have someone rooting you on to evolve because everyone is not willing to put in the work nor willing to face themselves. So, you must be different and go against the odds. Think about you for a moment. **You were created.** If you thought about the beauty that lies within knowing that statement it would give you goosebumps. If it takes action to create you, then it must take action to evolve.

The very first step in evolving is making the choice that you will evolve. And that is not always easy because you must continue to stay focus, when test and old thoughts rise, when people fall away from you, when you question yourself on if you're doing the right thing. It's not a matter of what rises. It's about what you choose to do when they do rise. That's why it is a priority to know why you're evolving. Because anything can blow you away. And if you are blown away easily, you won't get a chance to see all the fruition evolving has for you. Secondly, evolve in the way you want to evolve. If you know without a doubt the work that you are doing is shaping you into a better person. Continue to do what is working for you. Lastly, imagine what evolving could look like for you if you keep at it. Evolve to become a better person and have fun with burning down old truths. The time is now for new truths to rise from the old ashes.

The learning phase is huge because you can learn from a variety of things. Which is fascinating. There is power in any and everything you learn. Life is here to offer the best things to you so why not expand your perspectives and expectations? What a shame to go through this glorious life that God has given you and never live up to the highest version of yourself. And what better time do you have than right now? You can feed on baby food levels because you can learn from all levels. But don't stay on the baby food level forever. You may ask, how do I know when it's time to move on to another level? Your instincts will tell you and your desires will change. And every level you pass, there is always a new level to be exposed to.

Raise the bar when it comes to everything concerning yourself and owning your life. Learning is a process because anytime you are learning something you may have to study it for a while so the understanding can marinate within you. I challenge you to learn on as many levels as you can. Learning is infinite and anytime you withhold yourself from learning new things you teach yourself that you are incapable of retaining information. You are capable of anything. Always remind yourself that you are infinite.

The learning phase is exciting because when you gain new understandings, you speak to yourself differently, you gain new ways to respond, you gain enlightenment, attitudes change, and you weigh giving your energy to certain nouns. It is always interesting to be able to move away from a version of yourself that you use to know. You can look back on your own growth and when you are learning new things for yourself, it doesn't matter what others are saying about you. Because you know you are changing and gaining new knowledge to become a better you.

Once you have soaked in new understandings, I encourage you to teach others what you have been learning and create a domino effect. Don't be selfish when you find out new things. SPREAD THE WORD. Sometimes those you are around may not have the capacity to teach you things. So instead of going without the teachings, introduce yourself to old philosophers, speakers that fuel you and supportive people. Authentic people don't mind teaching you what they have already been through because they are happy that they made it through and before you ask, yes, it's important to be aware of the teachings you are tuning into.

There is always a deeper picture in seeing you and how you are operating in life. Everyday has something to teach you which means you have something to teach others. The days of our lives are expressed in teachings we expose ourselves too. And its selfish to go through something, come out better, and refuse to tell others about it. Sometimes people feel like they are the only ones suffering until they hear another man or woman tell their story. When you listen to stories and how people were able to free themselves, it teaches you that we all go through things, allows you to look at things you go through, and shows you that people may be going through worse. We can get together, share what we have gained, and create atmospheres of real change.

Teaching is and always will be infinite. Don't worry about looking your best when you begin your teaching journey. People are moved by what comes out of your mouth more than what you have on. The goal is to teach and share your truths in hopes to help someone else. And sometimes you may be teaching someone something and you end up helping yourself. The root lies in being a teacher to yourself first. Because when you fall, and you don't have time to remember what someone else taught you, it is a must that you have enough substance from within to teach yourself how to get up. Always remain true, passionate and never forget that your teachings are powerful and carry the ability to help someone else.

Once you hit the ADAPT phase, you are in the zone of fresh opportunities. It will take time to adapt to your new way of being, and that is okay. Please do not get discouraged. When your mind has been operating under the same system for so long, it is expected for you to be uncomfortable. Don't look for things to be comfortable when you are uprooting a new system. Everything is not meant to be easy, and you must continue to work at yourself and nurture the new and authentic version of who you are.

Adapting introduces your new design and leads to you seeing yourself in a new way. Allow God to call you away and show you what you made of. God is for you, and He loves to see you operating at your best self. God is the main ingredient who helps you along the adapting phase. If you feel like the journey is not working, recenter yourself. Don't forget about all the progress you have been making. Seeing all the work you have been doing and adapting into the new version of yourself is one of the greatest feelings. In a world where there is always something going on, YOU stand know who you are, and you walk in it.

You will stick out like a sore thumb because you are behind the scenes putting in work others are not willing to put in. Don't complain about what you don't like about yourself if you're not willing to change anything. Adapting is turning away from all the excuses that did revolt against you, taking yourself by the hand and telling yourself, "THIS IS MY TIME TO SOAR!" Stand boldly with the new you, remain humble and always give thanks unto God that you found your fight from within. Because the harsh reality is, some people will never do what is necessary to adapt into the best version of themselves.

Do you believe DELTA is worthy of building on? You owe it to yourself to discover, evolve, learn, teach, and adapt into becoming better and engaging in a better way of living.

"One day, the caterpillar stops eating, hangs upside down from a twig or leaf and spins itself a silky cocoon. The caterpillar radically transforms its body within its protective casing, eventually emerging as a butterfly," (Jabr, 2012). Butterflies are the embodiment of transformation. So, you understand that a butterfly must start out in one form to become another. Stay in your process so you can see what you can become.

Writing Prompts

What is holding you back? List five things that are holding you back from seeing who you were designed to be:
1._____
2._____
3._____
4._____
5._____

Now, serve each one an eviction notice. Make it clear that today is the last day you will allow any of these things to hold you back.
_____
_____
_____
_____
_____
_____
_____
_____
_____
_____
_____

Affirmation

I can discover, I can evolve, I can learn,
I can teach and I can adapt to a higher
awakening of myself

CHAPTER 7
KEEPING COMPANY WITH GOD

Keeping company with people in your life is easy because you can talk on the phone, email one another, text, facetime, have brunch dates, and take vacations. There are many ways to keep company with those you want to keep company with. But how do you keep company with a God you cannot see? God must be experienced. God does not need you to be perfect, nor do you need to know all the right things to say to keep company with Him. God is all about you being yourself and bringing all of you to the table. You know how you go on dates and put on decent clothes and only show your date the side you want them to see? And you're doing that so you can impress the person. Not realizing that you are teaching yourself that it is priority to impress someone else before you impress yourself. That is why you must be clear on your intentions when you meet people. Because God blesses intention.

How do you build a relationship where dishonesty lies in the root? Remember everything begins as a root and if you are building a foundation in any relationship you always want it to come from good ground. Keeping company with God when you come to Him naked is when He does His best work. And it also teaches you how to be honest, grounded, and upfront with yourself. If you cannot be honest with yourself, you cannot be honest with anyone else. It is in keeping company with Him where you find out how infinite you are. God is the only one that knows exactly how you feel during the good and bad days, high energy, low energy, and no energy days. Yes, you can encounter people that will be there for you but not in the way that He can. Remember God must be experienced because God is everything and more.

Imagine waking up one morning and it is raining outside. As you see the rain come down, you begin to witness beautiful babies descending from the sky in raincoats. The raincoats are so protective that the babies are not getting wet at all. Once the babies land, they have scrolls and the scroll reads: **God cannot be explained; he must be experienced**. The babies kiss you on the forehead and ascend back into the sky. It would blow your mind. In the day we live in, people would hurry to get their phones to record it and phone calls would be made. All social media platform lives would be going crazy. You would be calling up your friends telling them to go outside. Screaming in the phone saying, "It's babies coming down from the sky bringing notes saying God must be experienced and explained!" You know how you do when you are excited and start reading things the way you see them written! Journalists, news reporters, private investigators, cops on stakeouts, etcetera, would all be beyond shocked. It would be the new hot topic. Businesses would capitalize on it, and it would be an inspiration for some. But the bottom line is there will be a lot of activity going on. So even though you have been exposed to this unparallel experience, how do you unravel the message? God cannot be explained; He must be experienced. You must keep company with him and don't be surprised when God begins to show you what you are made of.

"I am the vine, ye are the branches: He that abideth in Me, and I in him, the same bringeth forth much fruit: for without Me ye can do nothing," (John 15:5 KJV).

This is the scripture I chose to memorize back in high school. It made me feel good to know that I knew at least one scripture. But one day I wanted to understand what the scripture meant. He is the vine; I am the branch. That lets me know that I am not in control, and it is not about things going my way. I am a branch, and the branch lane is where I stay. Everything has a system and when I decide to switch the roles up and think I am the vine and God is the branch, I mess up the system.

If He abides in me and I in Him, now I see that God is for stability. I cannot be all over the place and expect God to abide in me. God will not abide with anything that is unstable because He is for partnership. God will bring forth much fruit when I remain stable. When you keep company with God. You find out that you are not only remaining stable and waiting to receive fruit. God wants to see if you can remain stable when hell is breaking loose, and you don't know what is going on. GOD WILL TEST YOU. And He wants to see when you are up against things, what will you do. No doubt God will bring forth the fruit but not before the test.

Then He tells me in the end, without Him I can do nothing. That is precisely what happens when I choose to do things the way I see fit. I am left with the symptoms of being worried, stressed, feeling stuck, anxiety is through the roof, asking people to tell me what I should do when I'm supposed to be talking to Him. After about a thousand times of me being frustrated with doing things without Him, I came to myself and I told myself no matter what, I will remain in company with Him always. I AM NOTHING without Him. I can't stand, move, breathe, or think without God. I have no life, I don't evolve, I can't heal and without him I will never see who I am destined to be.

God has always been with me even in the moments where I felt like I had no one. And I didn't always know He was there. But when I look back and see all the moments I endured where I thought I was going to break, God was right there with me. Remember I told you, the worst place to be is caged in your mind. And I spent many nights witnessing how my thoughts were trying to cage me in. I challenge you to experience Him for yourself. God is in a lane ALL by Himself. GOD IS CHANGE.

The fact that I can hug myself and give myself love like I never have before, lets me know that God has revolutionized things down on the inside of me. Keeping company with Him allows me to be a better version of myself. I don't have to walk through life afraid or ashamed. And I understand that just because my life started out one way. It does not mean that is how it must end. Hooking yourself up to God is the best relationship to obtain. It's not about going to church to obtain a relationship with Him. It's deeper than that because God is a deep God. He goes past the surface, and it is only when you decide to keep company with Him that you find out how deep He is.

There was no manual that I read on how to gain relationship with Him. I simply began talking to Him like I would a friend. Keep company with Him and see for yourself and you won't regret it. GOD IS THE REAL DEAL. And God is for real relationships and encountering real connections.

The way I spoke on the babies earlier exemplifies God pulling a thought out of my head, which allowed you to imagine what I was describing. Never forget that you and I are co-creators with the creator himself, and God wants to reveal things unto you. You are full of all kinds of treasures and ideas. And when you keep company with God. He will slowly show you all that you are made of.

I have had moments where I have written letters to God, and if you wonder why, it's because I love and I'm in love with Him. I have no shame about it. I stand and trust Him because I know He always does things in my best interest. God is my protection, my peace, my shield, my laughter, my hope, my joy, my morning, my night, my shooting star, my rock. God is everything and I encourage you to hide and seek Him so, you can have a relationship of your own. It does you no good to only hear what God is to me and not dive into the ocean for yourself. Even if you don't know how to swim, God will be your life jacket. Strip yourself and dive in.

Writing Prompts

What is holding you back from keeping company with God? List five things that are holding you back from where you want to be:
1._____
2._____
3._____
4._____
5._____

Now, serve each one an eviction notice. Make it clear that today is the last day you will allow any of these things to hold you back.

_____
_____
_____
_____
_____
_____
_____
_____
_____
_____

Affirmation

GOD
PLEASE
OVERSTAY
YOUR WELCOME

CHAPTER 8
Crack Your Egg to Get to Your Yolk

When you crack an egg, do you ever take a moment to look at how vibrant the yolk is? I learned the color of the yolk comes from how well the chicken is being fed. People have come up with so many unique ways to use an egg. Eggs can be scrambled, sunny side up, poached, fried, baked, or boiled. Eggs are packed with so many health benefits ranging from repairing body tissues, carrying lots of vitamins that the body needs, minerals for the brain and they help the nervous system to function. YOLKS ARE INFINITE. It takes twenty-four to twenty-six hours for a chicken to hatch an egg. You can see the significance and the power that lies in the yolk. Because God designed the chicken to release the egg with a protective coating, you don't see the yolk until the protective coating is cracked. *Note to self, God will always protect anything that carries power.*

Even though some chickens aren't in the best setting to hatch an egg, they still carry yolks that hold power. Just because you don't see your power doesn't mean you don't have any. The yolk has always been down on the inside of you, it was just covered in confusion.

Now is the time to begin to get rid of everything that is covering your yolk and keeping you away from seeing your power so, you can see how vibrant you are. When will you crack your egg to get to your yolk? You can look at yourself for a moment and see that God decided that skin was going to be your protective covering. But He still wants you to crack yourself open and see all the power and beauty that lies within.

Dr. Thema is someone that can help you get to your yolk, and she can be found on SoundCloud. The grace that she carries when she speaks is something to lay down in. On her very first episode, she speaks about coming home to yourself and what it means to be home within you. It is one thing to have truth meet you in the face and not do anything about it, and it is another to meet the truth and change. Even though you have skin as protective coating, life, people, situations, and past mistakes have the power to damage your yolk. And sometimes you can be in your own way of getting rid of the damages. But I challenge you to remove everything that needs to be removed so, you can see the power that lies within you.

People would tell me that I was doing things but because I did not want to listen or own up to what I was doing, I denied, denied, denied. People would say that I cared too much about what others think. And I knew this to be a truth, but I did not want to own up to it. All denying did was keep me enslaved to not owning up to what I was dealing with. I was blinded for a long time with admitting my wrongs. I had to come to myself and fix what needed service. If you have different people telling you the same thing, then take time to assess you and get you right so you can own you in a refreshed way. Honesty with God and to yourself is vital. I understand that if I can lie to myself, I can lie to someone else. Next time someone says, "I would never lie to you," ask them if the same applies to themselves.

Sarah Jakes Roberts has a sermon titled *Wet Wood Still Burns*. Even though I listen to her other sermons, podcasts, and clips of her messages on social media platforms, this one is a sermon I can never forget because of the significant hold it had on me. The sermon made me realize that God will have His way with me no matter what I am dealing with. God does His best work when I come with everything I am. He knows what and how to clean me up. I see now it was His mission for me to go through everything I went through. I didn't like what I had to endure, nor did it make me feel good. But I am better now that I cracked my egg and began to do the work that was needed. I don't have to live life afraid, insecure, trying to fit in, being in denial, pointing fingers at people, not healing, and blaming because I am free from all those things, and I can move freely and live out my life's purpose.

Sarah mentions when you have the option to choose between power and fire, you better choose fire. Even though power may shift things, only fire can burn it up. I thought I needed more strength. I was wrong, I needed to work through my issues. I asked God to send down a fresh fire because I wanted those things that held me to my past, that held me to stinking thinking, kept me staying the same, held me to fears, and had me fighting with myself, to be removed. You will never see the power that dwells down on the inside of you if you don't work through what needs to be dealt with. So, I found myself as Sarah continued to preach stretched out on the floor with tears rolling down my face because all while I was crying, I could feel my soul on fire, and it occurred to me that I was the wet wood that could still burn. I thank God for downloading that message in her spirit. And I was home at the right time to receive it. That was a prophetic word and that message led me to see myself wet and burning, and I am forever grateful for the fresh fire that took place on that night.

Out of all the jobs I have worked, Dominos was the job that cracked my egg. At the time, I didn't realize that it did, but once I began to reflect on the moments that cracked my egg, my Domino's experience came to mind. I applied and was hired for a delivery position and my duties when I came in the morning were to prep food and help get the store open. My shifts were usually nine a.m. to seven p.m., Tuesday through Friday, and some Friday nights, I would work from nine until. Friday nights were one of our busiest nights, and my boss needed all hands-on deck.

Overtime, my boss saw something in me to express an interest in becoming a GM within the six months of me being there. Although I was excited that she trusted me with that position, my goals were doing what I needed to do and learning everything I needed to learn to make her proud. Sometimes I would work over my ten-hour shifts because it was short staffed. I didn't mind though because I was loyal, and I never liked to feel as if I was leaving her hanging. I remember one time it was so busy I had gotten off from working a ten-hour shift, and a dinner rush came out of nowhere all while being short staffed. So, I texted her and asked if she wanted me to go back in. She said if I didn't mind, she would greatly appreciate it. So, I went back in and helped until the rush died down. She thanked me in person again and gave me a gift card and I was honored that she did that.

Note to self, God always wants to see how loyal you can be to someone else's business before He blesses you with your own.

Anytime I could do something to be an asset, you could count me in. However, things began to shift when one of the coworkers told me that the boss and the manager I had been opening the store with were talking about me. I could not hold back asking them about what I heard but they both denied saying anything. I was shaken up by it all. It took about two days to process things, and in those two days, I decided that I would put in my two-week notice. I began to hear from other coworkers that the manager was telling the boss I was doing things that were not true. Me and this girl practically worked the same shifts so in my mind, I couldn't understand why she would do that. But it was not for my understanding at all.

When I cracked my yolk, I saw that I was teaching myself if everything was running smoothly, I was okay. But the first sign of things not going the way I thought they were supposed to go, I ran. People told me I was running but I didn't see it that way. I was focused on my feelings and principle. I felt as if I had been disrespected and my services were no longer needed. But the chatter did run me away. And until I learned how to stand in the mist of adversity and continue to focus on my work, God would present it in something else until I could pass the test of not running. From that moment on, I told myself I would never run from a situation again because of my feelings or focusing on who likes me and who does not. It was time to get comfortable in chatter, people not liking me or not always agreeing with me, even people lying on me and remain focused on what I was doing.

Cracking eggs may reveal what you don't like. But if you're still breathing you can work on anything that does not align with making you better. No matter what life brings, you must go through some cracking. Whatever cracking you may go through, learn what is needed, remove it from your yolk and move forward for the better. Decide that you will change for the better no matter what and go through all the actions necessary to hold yourself accountable. Don't allow tumors to form on your yolk. Get rid of and grow from anything that keeps you away from your highest self.

Writing Prompts

What is holding you back from getting to your yolk? List five things that are holding you back from where you want to be:

1._____
2._____
3._____
4._____
5._____

Now, serve each one an eviction notice. Make it clear that today is the last day you will allow any of these things to hold you back.

_____
_____
_____
_____
_____
_____
_____
_____
_____
_____
_____

Affirmation

I have dreams hope clarity peace joy
in my yolk and I will crack myself open
to let everything run out that is within me

CHAPTER 9
Get Up and Open the Curtains

You will never understand the experience of growing pains, until you allow God to work in you. It is very uncomfortable but very necessary. Everything you have received up to this point has been about process and the work that you must be willing to apply to yourself. And now that you have remained faithful over your work, it is His turn to have His way with you. He didn't get in your way when you were working, so don't get in His. Remember, I told you God is for partnership and when He sees that you have brought your fifty percent to the table, now, He can bring His. And don't be surprised when what He brings doesn't look like what you thought it would. The pressure He applies is so heavy, that you may not even be able to recognize yourself. It's time for Him to stretch you so you can reintroduce yourself. When I tell you that you don't have to remain the same, I mean that, beautiful.

God has been preparing you all along your process to be strong enough to bear growing pains. When God begins to apply pressure, it will be something that you have never felt before. **Don't crack under the pressure**. I know you don't realize it but through each moment you endured a process, God was watching you build your strength up. *Note to self, your growing pains will reflect the strength you were building in your process.* The pains are uncomfortable but take a moment and look back on all the changes that you have been making. Yes, this will be something new and painful, but it will be a new kind of pain. It will be a pain that hurts you for the better. If you didn't need the pain, God would have not applied the pressure to you.

If you don't get out of your way and endure what God wants to add to you, you miss the understanding of partnership, and you won't get the rest of the ingredients that you need to step fully into who you are becoming. Don't stop now that the pressing has begun and fall into the category of not operating in your highest potential. Please don't allow your feelings to get the best of you, everything is not always about feeling good. Pressure is the thing that is applied when it's time to get results, and results will always trump feelings.

The growing pains will not feel good. But you are aiming to reach the best version of yourself, do not lose sight of that. You are the one that must get up and open the curtains, but God is the one that is getting ready to show you the light He has been preparing you for. And He designed the light to shine in and through you. He didn't prepare the light that is for you five mins ago. It has always been there. But now you have matured, and He can trust you with the light. No progress, no light. No progress, no growing pains. No partnership, no new version of yourself.

The Philadelphia Orchestra performs Price: Symphony No. 3 in C minor: ll. Andante ma non troppo, (Nézet-Seguin, 2021). It is a beautiful performance to watch. The beauty of the performance allows you to see the work everyone had to put in to perform on the level that they did. Everyone had to show up for themselves individually and everyone had to show up ALL together. The stunning performance that was displayed before the audience was the light that God was preparing them for so, they all could see what

He was holding. He already knew how the performance was going to turn out before they did. But they all had to go through the countless practices individually and together to perform in the magnitude that they did. I am telling you; God holds His end of the bargain when you hold yours. Anything that has the power to become bigger than you is constantly worked on behind closed doors.

Progression in becoming your best self is not easy, and it takes countless acts of work to open yourself up. Therefore, you can't do it alone. You carry what you carry, and God carries what He carries and soon enough you will see the light. At the end or beginning of some performances, they may open and close the curtains. In the beginning, it is to reveal what is getting ready to happen and when they close the curtains, it indicates the show is over. But when you think about opening the curtains throughout your life, you must understand that it is not as simple as something opening or closing. A real revelation from opening your curtains comes from painful moments, enduring processes, and making sacrifices. You are the diamond under the pressure, never forget that. Yes, you may be left in awe of the performance but it's at the expense of the individuals being pressed, going through countless trials and test. Don't think for a second that they didn't have moments where they didn't FEEL like practicing. But what they were after trumped their feelings. And what God was holding in His hand allowed the audience to experience something unimaginable.

When you are transforming from one version of yourself into a new one, expect growing pains. Stepping into a new version of yourself is your fifty percent. What begins to produce when God throws his weight around in your life? Well, you must wait and see what will be revealed. Not excusing the fact that God was never there with you while you were putting in your work and shifting through your processes, because God is always with you. But what He has prepared for you, His fifty percent is revealed in stages. Your responsibility is to dive into all the treasures that are inside of you. Focus on being intimate with you first before you seek it out from another, build your character, have standards, build boundaries, understand you as much as you can in a loving way. Be aware of your thoughts without allowing them to control you. Stay focused, drink plenty of water, exercise your body and your mind. Try to feed anything that is a part of you and stay plugged into those that are in the direction you want to go. Thank God for being your closest friend and breathe through those growing pains.

God will reveal things to you before you are in a place where you want or think YOU should be. If you're connected to someone that does not fulfill you, learn the lessons that are wrapped up in it and move forward. For example, if you meet someone and both of you relate because of your mutual pain, and you start building a relationship from that, that is a root. Anything that is grown from that root sets the tone of the relationship. But one day something on the inside of you begins to awaken and you have a change in desires. You no longer want to be how you've always been; you no longer want to sell the old story to justify behaviors, you no longer want to be the person you see, you no longer want to build from a broken place. You decide in that moment that you will go through what you must to see yourself in a new way. Not knowing that change is painful because you have never stretched yourself. Not knowing that when you grow from one level to the next, you will experience growing pains.

God, action, fight, and consistency brings forth change. When you know who you are, you know who you are not. Know the power that lies in choosing and learning from different things. Always remember to see people for face value. If you remain in a growing stage, then yes teach them what you have been learning, but do not overstep. When action is applied to anything you will see the fruition in due time. Your job is to stay focused, have tunnel vision, and remain humble. We all have our own curtains that we must get up and open. You can't cut into someone else's process or try and make people change. Don't do that, allow people to evolve how they evolve and focus on what God is getting you prepared for.

February 12th, 2022, I took a flight to Rhode Island, and the pilot announced when we were 10,000 feet in the air and when we were 30,000 feet in the air. While I am on the plane, I take a moment to look down. I see the land, the cars, eighteen wheelers, and birds but everything was looking so small. From the plane the cars and eighteen wheelers look like small toy vehicles you can buy in the store. I said to myself, "If the world looks like this from this angle, is this how the world is viewed in God's eyes?" Then I got to thinking if the world really is this small. That means problems and situations that I allow to overpower my mind serve as distractions and I should not allow myself to get wrapped into things that I cannot control.

The real focus lies in seeking out who I am, seeing the beauty in the world, learning, growing, teaching, being who God created me to be, standing and flowing in my purpose and staying connected to that. I began to understand why the earth is His footstool, and God's thoughts must be above mine. The land was given to be walked on freely, and when you have begun to find yourself and your purpose, you don't have a choice but to build, because God is a building God. Look at all the work you have done. **Don't stop now**. Anytime distractions rise, I encourage you to tell the situations and distractions, that they are small, and they have no control over you or your life.

If an action must be taken for you to open the curtains on your life, it will take action for you to be in the flow of who God created you to be. Don't teach yourself to want anything better in life when you are not willing to do what it takes to achieve it. It will cause you more pain to announce what you want and not apply the action that is needed to achieve what you desire. You're never alone and soon enough you will see what is behind the curtains. Don't put yourself into a place where you want to open the curtains before it's time to, because you will think what God has prepared for you offers you nothing. You must build your mind up and dive into habits that reflect who you are. Do your work step by step and endure your processes. God has not forgotten about you. What a shame it would be to roam throughout life without getting to the place where you open your curtains and see all that God has prepared for you. DON'T CHEAT YOU.

Writing Prompts

What is holding you back from allowing God to show you, his fifty percent? List five things:

1._____
2._____
3._____
4._____
5._____

Now, serve each one an eviction notice. Make it clear that today is the last day you will allow any of these things to hold you back.

Affirmation

I can get up
I will get up
and I know
God has something significant for me and my life

Chapter 10

Affirmations

The meaning behind affirmation is the action or process of affirming something or being affirmed, (Merriam-Webster's, 2022). If I were to attend a seminar and I raise my hand, the affirmation would be the speaker looking in my direction and choosing me. I wonder if I use that same "call and command" action in my life? How can I see affirmations as spark plugs in myself and use them throughout myself? The power of what an affirmation holds when it is applied allows me to see and understand the power in my words. My words become a part of my self-talk routine and begin to work as daily vitamins in my life.

If I don't apply action with my affirmations, I won't see the power that lies within the words that I speak. I can begin with this affirmation:

"I no longer invite past actions to take up ownership today."

But if I do not apply the affirmation whenever my past shows up and TESTS me, I miss out on the power of the affirmation. My words must work during the good and the bad moments. I can not only teach myself to survive on one level. God is balance and I become whatever God is. Which means I move and speak through anything that is thrown at me. I CANNOT BE BROKEN, BECAUSE GOD DESIGNED ME TO BE UNBREAKABLE.

When I turned twenty-eight on February 18th, 2022, I had a rush of exhilarating thoughts. This is the beginning of a new chapter. I was welcomed with beautiful energy radiating from within and I had the opportunity to be on a plane. I began telling myself new shifts are beginning to line up, and this will be the beginning of greatness activated, like hugging myself and being thankful that I love myself. All these thoughts and words that I began speaking to myself were holding power. When I began speaking words over my life, I thought my words were not working. But I learned that the words I speak in and over my life are where it all begins. Of course, it's a thought first but I must work my words as well. My words are valuable and so are yours. What I speak in and over my life does matter. What are you telling yourself about you?

Affirmations are spark plugs that lead YOU to run at the speed you were made to run on.

I am growing.
I am beautiful.
I love me.
I am made new.
I can stop giving life to the past.
I know my words are powerful.
I must be careful when I speak.
I have changed.
I am better.
I am wise.
I can own my life.
I can own me.
I can give myself a second chance.

God still has something waiting for me.
I am the gift wrapped up.
I am not my excuses.
I am the author of my life.
I can read something new.
I can listen to new things.
I can learn.
I can teach.
I can discover.
I can adapt.

These words began to flow into the grooves of my mind. Anytime I was speaking more positive affirmations over myself and no longer wasting my words with:

I can't do this.
It won't work out.
Why don't they understand me?
Why am I so invisible?
I don't fit in.

The more I added light thoughts, my dark ones began freeing themselves. I had to mix some action into them to move from one thought to another. Everything that comes from my mouth has power and no matter what condition I face through life, what I feed on I become.

What words are you saying to yourself?

Yes, I was the black sheep of the family and God knew I would get fed up with being in unhealthy energies sooner or later. God knew me before He placed me inside the womb. People cannot give you what they do not have within themselves already. That is a reality all within itself. And anything I didn't agree with I blocked with expectations in all areas in my life and I fell into this space of becoming my own best friend. But God came and we took walks together, we gazed at trees, we cried, we laughed, we built, we talked, we loved, we hurt. We were friends and I experienced a real connection. Affirmations lead to discovering more of who I am. And when I know more of who I am, I know who I am not. Affirmations are infinite and when you work them the new version of yourself slowly reveals. I dare you to begin applying affirmations and be radical enough to discover all that you are.

Affirmations lead to access granted. Unhealthy words I was using over my life were doing more damage than good. But those unhealthy words were only distractions because I realized I can change the way that I speak at any moment in my life. Things that were meant to consume me were ALL SMALL. What matters is me getting rid of all the funk and speaking good things into my life. Once I saw how dark thoughts were leaving my mind, I was slowly developing mental loops of light. While I was feeding myself with unhealthy affirmations, I was telling myself that I did not matter and that I was an accident but once I came to myself and begin to try something else, I felt lifted in what I was telling myself. My words were shifting how I was seeing myself, how I was showing up for me, shifting perspectives, allowing me to hear differently. God was needing me to understand low so I could appreciate good and not take it for granted. I don't regret anything I went through or put myself through. All of it was learning lessons and God was growing me so He could reveal the goodness that was waiting for me all along.

I was the master in procrastinating. I would say that I was going to start something and not finish it countless times. I grew tired of teaching myself that it was okay to not hold myself accountable. I stopped being all over the place and began to take myself and my words seriously. I asked myself what I could be producing right now, and God gave me the assignment to write my book and I decided that I would not give up on it no matter what. I stuck to it, and while I stuck to it, I began feeling good about producing something, experiencing growing pains, applying action, being frustrated, starting over. I was enduring all the processes I had to endure. To finish what I said I was going to finish. And through everything, it has been amazing.

Writing my book is by far one of the best things I have done, and even though I began writing a book, I had to get away from needing times or places to be perfect before I started writing. Yes, I was working, but I was still writing. Life is and always will be life. Which means there is no perfect time in beginning to take ownership of myself and my life. NO MORE EXCUSES. Chose to do a new thing and it will show you what you can become. God tested me to see if my word held weight when I didn't feel like it. Could I write on low energy days or could I only produce when I am flowing in good energy? Writing was helping me break excuses and each time I finished a chapter I was closer to getting to the next one until I was finished.

WAKE UP, WAKE UP, WAKE UP. You are free and you never have to be locked down to anything. If what you see outwardly is not feeding you inwardly, apply new words to yourself and work everything you speak. Don't worry about situations or distractions. Away with this foolishness of, "Oh well, I have been this way, so I can't change." It's stupidity at its finest, and anytime you speak out from rusty old pipes, you are speaking from an unhealthy position. While you have been in this position; you have taught yourself that this is it for you. I know because I have done it too. But God STILL wants to show you His plans.

I challenge you today to choose not to speak down on you. Think about it for a moment; words are power instruments. When someone uses words to encourage you, you are lifted, and when someone uses words to hurt you, you are torn down. What you say to yourself, what you allow others to say to you, the way you speak in and over your life, ALL MATTERS. Begin today by saying over yourself, "My words matter, I will, and I must change the way that

I speak to myself because this is my life. I am rooting for me, and God is rooting for me."

Day by day and night by night if you sow good words into yourself, with action, fight and consistency, you can build yourself up. God is with you always and God ALWAYS blesses intentions.

Writing Prompts

What is holding you back from speaking good words in and over your life? List five things that are holding you back from where you want to be:

1. _____
2. _____
3. _____
4. _____
5. _____

Now, serve each one an eviction notice. Make it clear that today is the last day you will allow any of these things to hold you back.

_____
_____
_____
_____
_____
_____
_____
_____
_____
_____

Affirmation

when I turn my words
into promises and speak them over me
I become the promise I speak

Conclusion

Once I decided to choose myself, take baby steps, and lock in on action, fight, and consistency, I began to grow and see myself as a new being. It was from stepping into the unknown version of myself that I was able to look back and realize that God was with me every step of the way. I had to get from under all the negative thoughts and speak over my life what and how I wanted to see myself.

Was it easy?

No.

Was it worth it and am I better for it?

Absolutely.

The more I heal the little girl within, the better she becomes. And we grow together. I have downloaded the updated version of myself in one form and I am excited to see how I continue to grow up within me. I always remain infinite because that is how God created me to be. I self-reflect, I reset, I dive into a new thing for thirty days, I remain alert to check engine lights, I take my stairs, I am DELTA, I keep company with God, I crack myself to reveal my yolk, I look forward to seeing what's behind my curtains, and I remain in a place of speaking goodness over myself and in my life.

About the Author

I'm still developing on the journey of discovering myself. I can tell you that I broke up with the issues of the past and the limitations that people placed on me and that I am following and trusting the rhythm and instincts God set in me. Download The Updated Version of Yourself is nonfiction, and this is my first book. I encourage you to journey with me because I realize how nerve-racking it can be to be naked with someone about personal experiences. But I'm convinced that God designed us to be intrigued by different writings. Sharing stories opens a spectrum of feelings such as hope, courage, change, inspiration, moments of expansion, self-reflection, wisdom, etc.; it is a rich form of connection. What I love about nonfiction is that it creates a space to speak the truth with hopes of allowing people to realize they are not dealing with life and circumstances alone.

Because life began one way for you and me, it does not mean life has to end the same way. Fresh thoughts with action, fight, and consistency will set you on the path of rebuilding yourself, which leads to rebuilding your life. No updated mind, no updated you, no updated life. It's impossible to operate efficiently with a caged sense; as I produce more books, you will gain your perception of me through my writing. I'm complex; I went through things and even put limitations on myself. But I will always refuse to settle for anything less than who I am and intend to own my life. I want to hear from you. You can reach me at ownyourlife444@gmail.com. Begin rebuilding YOU today because no one promised you that you could begin tomorrow. Love and Loyalty

NOTES

Self-Reflection
Wignall, N. (August 12th, 2019) *Know Thyself: 3 Essential Skills for Better Self Reflection*. Retrieved from https://nickwignall.com/self-reflection/
New International Version. (2011). Bible Gateway.com. https://www.biblegateway.com/passage/?search=romans+12%3A2&version=NIV
New International Version. (2011). Bible Gateway.com. https://www.biblegateway.com/passage/?search=2+corinthians+9%3A6&version=NIV

Resetting
Burnett, D, (December 21st, 2021) *Into The Mystic*. Retrieved from https://www.psychnewsdaily.com/1111-angel-number-meaning/#:~:text=The%201111%20angel%20number%20is,be%20answered%2C%20and%20aspirations%20achieved.
King James Version. (2011). Bible Gateway.com. https://www.biblegateway.com/passage/?search=Psalm+8%3A6&version=KJV

30-Day Mental Diet
Kinnear, W. (1963). *30 Day Mental Diet*. Science of Mind Publications: DeVorss & Company.

DELTA
Jabr, F. (2012, August 12th). *How Does a Caterpillar Turn Into a Butterfly?* Scientific American. https://www.scientificamerican.com/article/caterpillar-butterfly-metamorphosis-explainer/#:~:text=One%20day%2C%20the%20caterpillar%20stops,as%20a%20butterfly%20or%20moth.

Keeping Company With God
King James Version. (2011). Bible Gateway.com. https://www.biblegateway.com/passage/?search=John+15%3A5&version=KJV

Crack Your Egg to Get to Your Yolk
Roberts, Sarah. (2021) *Wet Wood Still Burns https://www.youtube.com/watch?v=WUJFlr6mXmo*

Get Up and Open the Curtains
Yannick Nézet-Seguin & The *Philadelphia Orchestra* (2021, October 21st) *Price: Symphony No. 3 in C Minor.* https://www.youtube.com/watch?v=jI6qZFrsDnw

Affirmations
Merriam-Webster.com (2022) Affirmation Definition & Meaning - Merriam-Webster

www.ingramcontent.com/pod-product-compliance
Lightning Source LLC
Chambersburg PA
CBHW032016290426
44109CB00013B/686